DIANA
PRINCESS OF WALES

DIANA
PRINCESS OF WALES

Julia Delano

SMITHMARK

This edition published in 1993
by SMITHMARK Publishers Inc.
16 East 32nd Street
New York, New York 10016.

SMITHMARK books are available for bulk purchase for sales promotion and premium use. For details write or telephone the Manager of Special Sales, SMITHMARK Publishers Inc., 16 East 32nd Street, New York, NY 10016, (212) 532 6600

Produced by Brompton Books Corp.,
15 Sherwood Place,
Greenwich, CT 06830

ISBN 0-8317-5163-0

Printed in Hong Kong

10 9 8 7 6 5 4 3 2

CONTENTS

PAGE 1: *The Princess of Wales in the delicate Spencer family tiara which she also wore on her wedding day, here matched with drop pearl earrings.*

PAGE 2: *Diana in one of the elegant fitted two-piece suits she favours for daytime engagements.*

LEFT: *Attending the opening day of Ascot in 1987 with her sister-in-law, the Duchess of York.*

CHAPTER 1

FROM PONYTAIL
TO PRINCESS

ABOVE: *The glamorous Georgiana Spencer (1757-1806), daughter of the first Earl Spencer, married the Duke of Devonshire and also had a much-publicised affair with the then Prince of Wales, later George IV.*

RIGHT: *Solo princess, spring 1993; Diana presents the McDonalds Children of Achievement awards.*

The end of a fairytale or a new beginning? The announcement on 10 December 1992 that the Prince and Princess of Wales were to separate, but not divorce, was received with sorrow but no great surprise, and finally put an end to several years of increasingly intrusive media speculation. There is nothing new in an unhappy royal couple living apart, and the unhappiness of both Diana and Charles in each other's company had been painfully apparent for some time – notably during the disastrous Korean tour which was supposed to reflect a reconciliation. What is new is Diana's determination to retain her independent life as a full-time career princess and to demonstrate that the role she created for herself during twelve years of increasingly distant marriage is performed in her own right and not as her husband's wife.

There was little in Lady Diana Spencer's background to suggest that she would develop quite so far between the ages of 20 and 33. She was born on 1 July 1961, the youngest of Earl and Countess Spencer's three daughters. The Spencers really wanted a son and heir to carry on the name and title, and Diana's mother was put under considerable pressure to take medical advice about her tiresome propensity to have daughters. The longed-for son, Charles, now Earl Spencer since his father's death in March 1992, was finally born three years later.

The first-known Spencer was an extremely successful sheep trader in the fifteenth century, and his successors accumulated a substantial fortune, earned an earldom from Charles I and built Althorp House in Northamptonshire. The family remained loyal, dependable and conventional courtiers for three centuries, linked by blood to Charles II and the Dukes of Marlborough, Devonshire, and Abercorn. Technically, in fact, Diana Spencer's family has more royal blood in its lineage than does the House of Windsor.

The marriage of Viscount 'Johnny' Althorp, as he then was, and the Honourable Frances Roche, daughter of Baron Fermoy, was the society wedding of the year in 1954. Frances, at 18, was the youngest girl this century to be married in Westminster Abbey, and the Queen, the Duke of Edinburgh, and Princess Margaret were among the 1700 guests. Sadly, what began as a love match ended

Lin Pac Plastics
Suppliers of Hot Pack
to Mc Donald's.

and producers of meat & produce trays eggboxes
disposable tableware, horpacs, vistapac & film

would like to congratulate th
ildren of achiev

in an acrimonious and contested divorce when, in 1966, Frances met and fell in love with the flamboyant and extrovert Peter Shand Kydd. Her hope that she would be allowed to keep the two youngest children, then six and four, were shattered when her own mother, Ruth, Lady Fermoy, testified against her during the hearing of the case.

Diana was brought up in comfortable, indeed privileged, circumstances at Park House in Norfolk, conveniently close to Sandringham, although, contrary to some reports, the family were not on close terms with the royals. After their mother's departure, Diana and her young brother Charles were cared for in Norfolk by a series of nannies while the two older girls, Sarah and Jane, went to a Kent boarding school. All the children continued on a regular basis to see their mother, who initially lived in London, and there was the inevitable

rivalry between divorced parents vying for the affection of their young.

Diana's early teenage years produced an unremarkable educational record; her desire to be a ballet dancer was foiled by her height. In 1975 the family left the familar comfort of Park House for the more forbidding splendour of Althorp when, on the death of his father, Johnny Althorp became the eighth Earl, his son became a Viscount, and his daughters all became Ladies. Further upheaval was caused by his remarriage in 1977 to the former Countess of Dartmouth, daughter of the saccharine romantic novelist Barbara Cartland. The formidable Raine Spencer has successfully turned Althorp into a paying proposition in order to meet the crippling debts that the new Earl had inherited, but she was not a wholly welcome addition to the family.

School for Diana was followed by the traditional Swiss

LEFT: *When Diana's parents married in Westminster Abbey in 1954, it was the society wedding of the year.*

ABOVE: *Ruth, Lady Fermoy, Diana's maternal grandmother, deplored the break-up of her daughter's marriage, but has been a great support to her royal granddaughter.*

RIGHT ABOVE: *A charmingly informal photograph of Diana Spencer on her first birthday.*

RIGHT BELOW: *The young Diana with her brother Charles, the long-awaited heir and now Earl Spencer.*

LEFT AND BELOW RIGHT: *Diana had a typically comfortable and sheltered aristocratic upbringing.*

TOP RIGHT: *Earl Spencer married Raine, former Countess of Dartmouth in 1976.*

ABOVE LEFT: *The famous photograph of Diana as nursery teacher.*

finishing school, regarded by aristocratic families as the right way to prepare their daughters for the rigours of the social season and the still fairly standard search for a suitable husband. Living a sedate and rather sheltered life in London and weekending at Althorp and a succession of other substantial country seats, Diana did a number of fairly meaningless and menial jobs and babysat for her sister Jane, who married Robert Fellowes, now private secretary to the Queen, in 1978. It was sister Sarah who seemed to have the golden prospects, attracting the interest not only of the fabulously rich Duke of Westminster, but even of Prince Charles himself. Which is how Lady Diana Spencer came to meet the Prince of Wales in the middle of a field during a day's shooting on the Althorp estate in 1977.

It was a slow process. Diana moved from her mother's Cadogan Square flat to her own establishment in Earls Court, went skiing, worked as a dance teacher and then moved to the Young England kindergarten school in Pimlico, where she was in her element. In February 1979

she was asked to a Sandringham house party; in July she watched the Prince play polo at Cowdray Park; in August she was invited to join him on the royal yacht *Britannia* for Cowes Week; and in September she went for the first time to Balmoral for the Braemar Games. By then the press were in hot pursuit and had staked out the flat in Coleherne Court. Diana's flatmates acted as decoys, driving her distinctive Metro about London to allow their beleaguered friend some privacy in her developing romance.

The world's newspapers had already investigated the complete Spencer genealogy, discussed Diana's previous boyfriends (none of them, much to various editors' disappointment, remotely serious), and speculated endlessly about her chances before the engagement was formally announced on 24 February 1981. The previous six months had been an ordeal by media pack which taught the Princess some invaluable lessons, but the next five, before the wedding on 29 July, were to prove equally stressful.

As soon as the engagement was public, the royal system enveloped this 20-year-old kindergarten teacher. Leaving her Earls Court flat for the last time, Diana was taken by Rolls to Clarence House, home of the Queen Mother, moving on after a few days to the more large-scale and rigorous life of Buckingham Palace. The sudden and drastic change, and the difficulties Diana faced in coming to terms with the implications of marrying not just a Prince, but the heir to the throne, were visibly demonstrated by her dramatic weight loss in the months before the wedding. Her fears that the pressure of royal life would make it difficult to maintain contact with even the closest friends proved well founded. The magnificent ivory silk wedding dress had to be taken in several times in the course of the fitting process.

Every thing went off perfectly on the day, of course. The fabulous Glass Coach bore the bride and her father, still shaky from a stroke, safely and promptly to St Paul's Cathedral; the rain held off; the nation took a day's holiday and held its breath in sentimental delight; and Lady Diana Spencer married her prince and became a genuine twentieth-century Fairytale Princess. Perhaps the story should end there, but of course it does not.

LEFT ABOVE: *'It is with the greatest pleasure that the Queen and the Duke of Edinburgh announce the betrothal of their beloved son, the Prince of Wales, to Lady Diana Spencer, daughter of the Earl Spencer and the Honourable Mrs Shand Kydd'. So went the announcement from Buckingham Palace on 24 February 1981. Prince Charles had proposed and been accepted three weeks before, at a romantic private supper in his apartments at Buckingham Palace.*

RIGHT ABOVE: *A relaxed of Diana with her fiancée and future mother-in-law, taken at Buckingham Palace.*

RIGHT: *A delightfully casual shot of the engaged couple in robust country clothes, plus a camera-hogging Golden Labrador. Contrary to appearances, however, Diana was not a natural countrywoman, passionate about hunting, shooting and fishing, and this has proved an area of stress between husband and wife.*

ABOVE AND LEFT: *The famous strapless black silk taffeta dress, worn by Diana for her first evening engagement as the fiancée of the heir to the throne, earned the disapproval of the Queen Mother. Diana and Princess Grace of Monaco, another commoner who married royalty, found much to say to each other on the same occasion.*

FAR LEFT: *The actual moment of marriage, performed by the Archbishop of Canterbury, Dr Robert Runcie, in the words of the 1549 prayer book, although the bride firmly refused to promise to obey. Despite all the rehearsals, both made slight mistakes during the exchange of vows.*

ABOVE: *The wedding of the year, if not the decade, took place on 29 July 1981 in St Pauls Cathedral, rather than the more conventional Westminster Abbey. The soon-to-be Princess was up at 6.30 and enjoyed a large breakfast before being delivered into the hands of her hairdresser. She refused to have an elaborate lacquered hairstyle, and there were some who thought that her simple cut was a little too casual and fly-away under the delicate Spencer family tiara. The dress too created problems, not least the need to keep taking tucks in it as the pre-wedding stress told. Made of English silk and embroidered with tiny pearls and sequins, with wide frilled and scooped neckline and flouncy lace-trimmed sleeves, it was a dream of a wedding dress. The 25-foot long matching train and veil of ivory tulle gave the brides-maids a little trouble; here the youngest, Clementine Hambro (great-granddaughter of Sir Winston Churchill) and Catherine Cameron, follow the bride and groom out of St Pauls.*

LEFT: *Escorted by her father, a veiled Lady Diana Spencer enters the cathedral for the nerve-wracking 3½ minute walk to the altar, to the sound of massed trumpets playing Jeremiah Clarke's Trumpet Voluntary.*

RIGHT: *Leaving the Cathedral, the new Princess has thrown back her veil, dotted with ten thousand tiny hand-embroidered mother-of-pearl sequins, to reveal a cool exquisite face. Her cascading bouquet consists of yellow roses, freesias, lily-of-the-valley and a sprig of myrtle for luck.*

ABOVE: *A thousand doves fluttered up into the blue sky as the newly-weds travelled in their open carriage from St Paul's back down Fleet Street and the Strand to Buckingham Palace.*

LEFT: *Urged on by the enthusiastic crowd, Prince Charles first gracefully kissed his wife's hand and then, when that was not enough, her lips, the first ever public kiss on that balcony.*

ABOVE RIGHT: *The formal wedding photograph, taken at Buckingham Palace after the ceremony, shows the bride and groom surrounded by both families and a charming group of pages and bridesmaids.*

BELOW RIGHT: *The obligatory greeting from the palace balcony.*

CHAPTER 2

DIANA AS STYLE LEADER

RIGHT: *The Princess wears her mother-in-law's wedding gift to her, in turn inherited from Queen Mary: a diamond tiara with pendant pearls and a central lover's knot in French eighteenth-century style, which is saved for what the royals term a 'big dressing day'. Here it is matched with diamond and sapphire drop earrings.*

RIGHT: *A slimline and flattering fitted jacket in turquoise, a favourite colour, makes a practical outfit for a long day of public engagements and walkabouts. Diana invariably acquires an armful of posies whenever she meets the public.*

No one who saw the engagement photographs of Lady Diana Spencer, looking slightly plump in her unflattering blue suit bought off-the-peg from Harrods and peering shyly up from under her long hair, could have predicted that well within ten years she would be an international fashion leader and hailed as one of the world's best-dressed and most elegant women. The poise that comes with knowing that she is doing a difficult and demanding job well and has the ability to charm almost any audience has given Diana a much-needed sense of self-worth and an assurance that has further enhanced her natural good looks. In fact, at one stage in the long drawn out speculation about the royal break-up, a number of American fashion houses happily considered the possibility of offering the ex-

Princess of Wales a top modelling job. She herself, however, says that clothes are not her priority and is trying to cultivate a more serious image with her work as charity patron; to achieve something more tangible than simply looking good, which at one stage seemed to be all that was expected of her.

Just the same, her wardrobe is epic by any standard, and she is sometimes credited with reviving single-handed the flagging British fashion industry. A recent survey suggested that in the twelve years since her marriage she has spent close on £1 million ($1½ million) on clothes, and that does not take account of the private fun clothes she buys. She is the proud possessor of about eighty suits, fifty day dresses and over a hundred evening dresses, and there are matching accessories for every

LEFT: *To meet the Vienna Boy's Choir in April 1985, Diana wears a white coat dress with a deep black ruffle edging one side of the neckline, designed by Catherine Walker.*

ABOVE LEFT: *With Prince William at Aberdeen Airport on the way to Balmoral, wearing an elegant tailored coat with classic velvet collar.*

ABOVE RIGHT: *This ornate cream suit, with its tight skirt and jagged hemline, here seen as the royals wait at Victoria Station to greet the Spanish royal family, provoked fashion disapproval.*

outfit. Her clothes are planned weeks in advance and only a radical change of weather will prompt a change of plan. It takes two full-time dressers to organize the royal wardrobe, keeping a detailed record of what has been worn on each occasion. The size and sumptuousness of this collection of clothes does sometimes provoke critical comment; but then so do the occasions when she wears an already-familiar outfit once too often. Prince Charles was once asked teasingly by a cheeky photographer, 'Why can't you buy your wife a new frock then?'

The natural style of the nineteen-year-old Diana Spencer was that of any well-born young woman about town; striped shirts, Benetton sweaters, flat shoes, and hoop earrings. The house of Hartnell, who traditionally design elaborate, formal evening dresses for the senior royal ladies, held no attraction for her. Instead her sister Jane, who had worked at *Vogue* magazine as an editorial assistant before her marriage, introduced the princess-to-be to the *Vogue* fashion team: fashion editor Anna

Harvey, beauty editor Felicity Clark and former model Grace Coddington. They summoned clothes from designers' showrooms all over London for Diana to try, and encouraged her to develop her natural taste. The first sign that she was beginning to develop the confidence to establish her own style was the stunningly low-cut strapless black dress she wore to a formal dinner at the Goldsmiths' Hall, London, shortly before her wedding.

David and Elizabeth Emmanuel, who designed both the daring Goldsmiths dress and the gloriously romantic ivory silk wedding dress, have split up and vanished from the scene, but some of the top designers selected by the Princess in those early days have remained mainstays of the royal wardrobe. These include Jasper Conran, whose elegant wool suits are perfect for day, while his fun evening wear is ideal for less formal occasions. Catherine Walker of the Chelsea Design Company is another regular, and Rifat Ozbek and Victor Edelstein have both supplied glamorous evening gowns.

23

The Princess's favourite colours are still the rich, warm shades of red, purple, pink and turquoise that set off her blonde hair and tanned skin so well. She rarely wears man-made fabrics; in winter she wears wool jersey or wool crepe, which do not crease too badly, and in summer she prefers silk crepe to either linen or cotton. She has mastered all the secrets of the fashion trade; smoothing her skirt from the back and always wearing a silky petticoat to match her outfit. Skirts cannot be too short or, as she says 'When I bend over there are six children looking up it.' Hems may be weighted to avoid any possibility of the wind revealing more of the elegant royal legs than is thought seemly, and sleeves can also be a problem.

Diana's private wardrobe is a different matter altogether; when she is out with friends she sees no reason why she should not dress to please herself, and the result can be, to say the least, eye-catching – fake ostrich-skin jodphurs, for example, or brightly-coloured silk waistcoats from a men's outfitters. Sometimes her fun outfits have the fashion pundits sorrowfully shaking their heads, although they are usually gladly copied by the royal-watching public. The combination of black satin bomber jacket, ruffled blouse, red leather trousers and high heels which she wore for her third visit to Andrew Lloyd Webber's staggeringly successful musical *Phantom of the Opera* was generally agreed to be a disaster. Even on

couple of days of self-denial. Her make-up is simple and understated, concentrating on gold blusher (which also helps to disguise her tendency to flush when hot or stressed) and pink lipstick. Her main trademark is the line of sapphire blue eyeliner along the lower rim of her eyes, a tip picked up from ever-glamorous film star Elizabeth Taylor.

Jewellery is an essential feature of any royal lady's wardrobe, and Diana has been instrumental in making the wearing of extravagant, sometimes jokey, jewels trendy among the younger set with whom she mixes. The delicate tiara she wore for her wedding is a Spencer treasure; other wedding presents included Queen Mary's tiara in a lover's knot design of diamonds and pearls. Another Queen Mary jewel is the cabachon emerald and diamond Art Deco necklace which the Princess sported as a headband on one royal tour, when her neck was too sunburned to allow wearing it as a choker. Foreign tours often involve the giving of fabulous jewels, and some of Diana's most elaborate jewellery came from the Crown Prince of Saudi Arabia, who presented her with a stunning sapphire suite which included not one but two necklaces, one a sunburst pendant and one a choker. For less dressy occasions, Butler and Wilson in London's Fulham Road have supplied the fashion-conscious Princess with many a sparkling piece of diamanté.

formal engagements there is the occasional miscalculation, like the ornate cream suit with heavy gold braiding, tight skirt and v-shaped hemline that the Princess wore to the passing-out parade at Sandhurst Military Academy one year. And of course a single mistake causes far more comment than any number of classic, elegant outfits.

Diana has a streamlined and efficient beauty routine to ensure that she is always slim and exquisite. Swimming, workouts and a carefully controlled diet take care of her figure, which remains a desirable 34-25-36, and from time to time she signs herself in to a health farm for a

LEFT: *This memorable ensemble of polka dots, worn to a polo match, started a fashion trend.*

ABOVE: *Cool in flowing pale green silk and matching shady hat for a visit to Nigeria.*

RIGHT: *The Prince and Princess of Wales in nineteenth-century dress during a visit to the Klondike.*

LEFT: *Sometimes Diana's private fun style is allowed to influence her more formal wardrobe, as in this elegant matador-style trouser suit.*

ABOVE: *This black hat with its long face net has an appropriate air of solemnity for the Remembrance Day service.*

29

ABOVE: *For royalty hats are never out of fashion, but Diana's individual and stylish wearing of them has brought them back into vogue as a fashion accessory. This wonderfully zingy ensemble has graced a number of formal occasions.*

ABOVE: *A simple deep-crowned style. There are approximately 75 hats in the royal wardrobe, all kept meticulously stored in tissue paper and dust-free hat boxes. Initially the Scottish-born milliner John Boyd supplied most of the Princess's hats; more recently she has also patronized Graham Smith and Philip Somerville, who has created many of the larger and more sophisticated hats she wears now.*

RIGHT: *In Dubai in 1989 Diana chose her favourite skullcap-style overlaid with a wide flat white brim tilted rakishly over one eye, with suit to match.*

RIGHT: *Another delightfully cool confection in turquoise and white.*

ABOVE: *In Melbourne in 1988 the Princess wore a strapless pink and blue evening dress by Catherine Walker, split up one side and with a large bow flaring from the hip. Her pinned-back hair emphasized the magnificent diamond and sapphire jewels.*

ABOVE: *Black velvet and red taffeta combine in a dramatic flamenco-style gown with graduated hem and layers of black net underskirts; note the contrasting gloves, a daring and jokey touch!*

LEFT: *Diana in a heavy white satin dress with matching bolero jacket arrives at New York's 'Wintergarden' for a formal dinner in February 1989.*

LEFT: *A long knotted rope of pearls shows off the Princess's elegant back in a plunging crushed velvet dress, worn for the premiere of the film* Back to the Future.

ABOVE: *In Bangkok silk flowers make a change from a tiara, setting off the Princess's swept-back hairstyle and exquisite pearl drop earrings, and matching her fuchsia pink evening dress with its purple diagonal sash that falls into a train over one shoulder.*

ABOVE: *Before her marriage, Lady Diana Spencer favoured a three-strand pearl choker, seen frequently in 1980 and 1981, but this is a choker with a difference: a stunning seven-strand pearl creation with a huge sapphire clasp.*

RIGHT: *The Spencer tiara worn with the glorious sapphire and diamond jewellery which was a gift from the Saudi royal family.*

RIGHT: *Another magnificent choker worn with a glamorous red and silver gown for the* Hot Shots *premiere.*

DEVOTED MOTHER

ABOVE: *The doting parents leave hospital with Prince William.*

RIGHT: *Princesses too find pregnancy tiring; this blue cotton maternity dress by Catherine Walker, here seen at a polo match at Windsor in May 1982, was one of Diana's favourites.*

In conversation with veteran television personality Alastair Burnet in 1985, the Princess of Wales modestly described her role as 'supporting my husband whenever I can, and always being behind him, encouraging him. And also, most important, being a mother and a wife.' While it was painfully clear well before the separation that Diana no longer felt able to support her husband, there is no dispute whatever about the close and loving relationship between her and her two sons.

Within three months of marriage, Diana was pregnant. Like many women, she felt worst in the first few months, before her condition was obvious or a formal announcement had been made. A three-day tour of Wales in October 1981 was made miserable by morning sickness, and it was a relief when official confirmation of the pregnancy, on 5 November 1981, enabled her to discuss her condition with wellwishers. Prince William Arthur Philip Louis was born at 9.00 pm on 21 June 1982, in the private Lindo wing of St Mary's Hospital, Paddington, under the benign supervision of veteran royal gynaecologist George Pinker and with Prince Charles in anxious attendance. Within two years the Princess was pregnant again;

this time the announcement was made, rather touchingly, on Valentine's Day, 14 February, 1984. Henry Charles Albert David followed his brother into the world at 4.20 pm on 15 September, after a faster and easier labour. The boys' first names were Diana's choice, with Charles's preference for Arthur and Albert relegated to middle names.

Within the constraints of security and the royal schedule, Diana has tried to ensure that her sons live as normal a life as possible. In their early days they were cared for by the redoutable Barbara Barnes, an informal, independent-minded, and extremely experienced nanny who developed a good relationship not only with the boys but also with their mother.

It was Diana's suggestion that both William and Harry should attend nursery school, rather than the more usual royal pattern of employing a governess to educate them in the privacy of Kensington Palace in the early years. The choice of a school only a mile away, in Notting Hill, enabled the boys both to lead an almost normal school life and to see as much as possible of their parents. From there each moved on at the age of seven to Wetherby, a

select and expensive pre-prep day school. In autumn 1990 William moved on again, this time as a boarder, to Ludgrove preparatory school in Berkshire, to be followed by his brother two years later, leaving the Princess with an empty nest in Kensington Palace, at least in termtime.

The two family homes were Kensington Palace and Highgrove in Gloucestershire. The Kensington apartments will continue to be occupied by Diana and the boys when they are with her, while Charles remains at Highgrove with an apartment in Clarence House. Diana was influential in the redecoration carried out at Kensington Palace, and ensured that the bedrooms, nursery suite and two studies were kept cheerful, light and airy as befitted a family home; the formal reception rooms have a much more majestic and sombre tone.

The two princes are not the only junior residents of Kensington Palace. Their royal neighbours include Prince and Princess Michael of Kent and their two children, Lord Frederick and Lady Gabriella Windsor, and the Duke and Duchess of Gloucester and their three children, the Earl of Ulster, Lady Davina, and Lady Rose Windsor. Diana's sister Lady Jane Fellowes and her husband, the Queen's Private Secretary Sir Robert Fellowes, live in a grace-and-favour house nearby and their two daughters Laura and Alexandra are yet more company for their two princely cousins. There are so many royal children that when they were all younger, Diana considered setting up a kindergarten within the palace, and their cheerful presence adds immeasurably to its life and vibrancy.

The young princes also have their own private walled garden, which is well stocked with swings and climbing frames for the agile boys. Many an informal photographic session has been held here, but the Princess tries to protect her children from too much exposure to the media, telling them firmly that the photographers are more interested in her. Despite her attempts to prevent William, in particular, from being spoilt by the inevitable attention he gets, he has shown the occasional flash of royal arrogance. When he earned himself a cuff on the head from his mother at a school sports day in 1990, childcare experts were disapproving but other parents sympathised. There was also an alarming occasion when Prince William shot out of the door of the Waleses' apartment, straight into the path of a reversing Jaguar, to be plucked out of harm's way at the last minute by his furious and frightened mother.

When she is in London Diana tries to spend as much time with her sons as possible, despite her full working diary. In the days when both boys were at day school she would often reschedule her appointments so that she could meet them from school and then take them straight to Buckingham Palace for a swim in the royal pool. She also likes to do as much of their clothes shopping for them as she can, and can frequently be seen buying

ABOVE: *Prince Charles stayed with his wife throughout her difficult sixteen-hour labour and conducted her back to Kensington Palace less than a day later when she firmly decided she was ready to come home.*

RIGHT: *Prince William was christened in a small family ceremony in the Music Room in Buckingham Palace on the Queen Mother's eighty-second birthday. He let out three small protesting squawks when sprinkled with Jordan water by the Archbishop of Canterbury, but was soon soothed by a maternal finger.*

LEFT: *After Harry's birth Diana again left hospital within 24 hours, this time looking much more glamorous, in a red dress and shoes with red bows and with her hair blonder.*

ABOVE: *For Harry's christening the Princess, who is herself godmother to over 20 children, was able to choose more personal friends as godparents, including ex-flatmate Carolyn Pride and artist Brian Organ.*

matching shorts and sweaters in the junior Benetton in Kensington (she says that otherwise there are arguments).

The pace of life was more relaxed at Highgrove, and the Princess was able to enjoy the company of her children in a more homelike setting, but she is reported never to have felt fully at home there and escaped back to London whenever she could. The two princes are already promising horsemen, in the royal tradition, but their mother is less enthusiastic about the sport. Highgrove is a delightful eighteenth-century Georgian country house in a characteristically English style which is not dissimilar to Park House where Diana spent her childhood. It has a rambling garden with wildflower walks and fruit trees, an old-fashioned kitchen garden, and an organic farm in which Prince Charles takes a close interest. A rosemary hedge masks the swimming pool where the Princess used to take her daily dip.

Perhaps because they lived in such close proximity to other members of the royal family in London, the Waleses rarely invited any of them to Highgrove, although Princess Anne's country home of Gatcombe Park is only a few miles away. Diana has never enjoyed particularly close relationships with her royal in-laws, but she has grown closer to her own mother, the still glamorous Frances Shand Kydd, in recent years and has holidayed more than once in the Caribbean with her and the boys.

LEFT: *Some commentators were shocked when Diana insisted on taking the six-month-old Prince William on an extended tour of Australia and New Zealand, but she was determined not to be separated from her son for any length of time. Here the family pose for an informal photo call in New Zealand.*

ABOVE: *Prince William and his parents pose for photographers in the gardens of Kensington Palace; the one-year-old prince is well wrapped up against the autumn cold.*

RIGHT: *In the family apartment in Kensington Palace, now occupied by Diana alone, sometimes joined by her sons.*

LEFT: *Visiting the Niagara Falls, Canada, in October 1991, mother and sons are well protected against the spray.*

BELOW: *A thoroughly English tradition: the Mothers' Race at Sports Day. On the first occasion the competitive Princess won it, but this time she only came third.*

RIGHT: *A sombre occasion; Diana and the two princes are escorted from St Margaret's Church, London, after the memorial service in May 1992 for her father, who had died in March while the Waleses were on a skiing holiday in Lech, Austria. Earl Spencer had suffered a cerebral haemorrhage as long ago as 1978, from which he was nursed back to health by his second wife Raine.*

CHAPTER 4

DIANA AT PLAY

ABOVE AND RIGHT: *Ascot is a favourite social occasion and always finds the Princess looking her best and most relaxed. Here she is seen with the Duchess of York, another royal bride whose marriage went sour.*

The Princess of Wales has developed immeasurably in poise and self-assurance since the early days when the rigours of a public engagement could reduce her to private tears, and this is reflected very clearly in her determination to choose her own leisure activities. Constantly on display and playing a role in her working life, Diana recognizes the need to find time to relax and be herself, and has carefully built this into her working day.

The routine begins with a quick dash to Buckingham Palace for twenty or thirty brisk lengths, breaststroke, in the heated indoor pool. She returns with her hair still wet for a session with her regular hairdresser. Sometimes these early morning runs are extended to include the fulfilment of a personal ambition, such as visiting the BBC's television news studios or sitting silently in on the early morning show on Capital Radio, her favourite radio channel.

On an off-duty day in London, Diana's usual pattern is to spend the morning on royal business, first discussing future engagements with her equerry and lady-in-wait-

ing, then perhaps meeting officials from one of the charities she is involved with or studying sketches and samples for the royal wardrobe with one of her regular couturiers. She may slip out in jeans and a headscarf to do her own shopping, perhaps wheeling her own trolley round Safeway or visiting a local bookshop for the light novels she enjoys, though a discreet bodyguard will always be close by. She also goes regularly on more formal shopping trips, to Covent Garden and Bond Street as well as the smart Chelsea and Kensington stores favoured by rich young women.

If she is having lunch at home she may well invite a girlfriend to join her – one of a select group of true confidantes with whom she can enjoy a proper gossip. These include her former flatmates, Carolyn Bartholomew and Virginia Pitman, who have remained close friends of the Princess since the pre-engagement days when they loyally helped her dodge unwelcome media attention. Traditionally royalty have looked to the aristocracy for their immediate social circle, and Diana is no exception. Other close and trusted friends are Milly Soames,

daughter of the Lord Lieutenant of Herefordshire and her brother, banker Philip Dunne, James Gilbey, Kate Menzies of the publishing clan, Catherine Soames, and Lady Romsey. The Duchess of York was a regular visitor while she was still plain Sarah Ferguson and during the early days of her marriage, but the relationship cooled before the Yorks' separation was announced. Lunch is light, often vegetarian, with salads a must. Alternatively the Princess may meet friends at one of a number of favourite restaurants, perhaps Launceston Place in Kensington, Luigi's in Covent Garden or Green's in Mayfair, with the occasional foray to the Chinese restaurant Mr Wings for a change from traditional European cooking.

Other forms of relaxation include the occasional trip to the local Odeon cinema in Kensington High Street, or a comfortable night in front of the television. Favourite shows include Australian soap *Neighbours, Brookside*, chat shows – and the satirical show *Spitting Image*, which mercilessly lampoons the royal family among its many other victims. In the early days of her marriage the Princess earned the reputation of listening to nothing but pop music on her Walkman, but in fact her tastes are catholic, and she may equally well be listening to one of the great romantic composers such as Grieg, Schumann, or Rachmaninov. In her circle every well-brought up girl learns piano throughout her school career.

Fitness is almost an obsession with Diana; her dramatic weight loss both before her marriage and after William's birth was due as much to a rigorous exercise programme as to stress or dieting. Stress and fatigue are an inevitable part of the balancing act of being royal, however, and Diana combats them by keeping her body toned and supple. As well as regular swimming, she works out to a keep-fit video and does a regular dance routine, which she describes as a mix of jazz, tap, and ballet. There were some eyebrows lifted among the more traditional members of the royal circle when the Princess of Wales appeared on stage at Covent Garden in a routine choreo-

LEFT AND ABOVE: *Since Prince Charles is a keen polo player, Diana inevitably found herself, particularly in the early days of her marriage before she began to develop her own interests, spending some of her leisure hours watching polo matches. Here she rewards the winners; one of them with a kiss.*

graphed specially for her by ballet dancer Wayne Sleep, but no one could deny the quality of the performance.

Another form of exercise favoured by the sporty Princess is tennis, and she is a member of the exclusive Vanderbilt Club in Shepherds Bush, West London. Some discreet coaching has greatly improved her game, and she has enjoyed a much-publicised match with champion Steffi Graf, as well as more evenly matched battles with Julia Dodd-Noble, nicknamed Crown Jewels because she knows so many young royals.

Holidays were always a more delicate issue in the Waleses' household. Although the Princess was photographed at Balmoral during her honeymoon looking idyllically happy in her heathery Scottish surroundings, she is not enamoured of the hearty country routine of shooting and fishing that the royal family adopt on holiday. The Queen stays at Balmoral from early August, immediately after Cowes Week, until well into October, and other members of the royal family are expected to join her. Much more to Diana's taste is the week she and the boys spend each year with King Juan Carlos and Queen Sofia of Spain and their family in one of their summer homes. The favourite is the Marivent Palace in Majorca, overlooking the Palma yacht club, combined with leisurely sea cruises on the sumptuous Spanish royal yacht. Another holiday destination that is more to the Princess's taste is Princess Margaret's Caribbean hideaway on the beautiful and secluded island of Mustique.

TOP: *Balmoral is supposed to be a holiday, but there are inevitable social duties, such as the Braemar Games, which Diana enjoys less than some of her in-laws.*

ABOVE: *Scottish weather is notoriously unreliable.*

RIGHT: *Arriving at Aberdeen Airport on the way to Balmoral.*

ABOVE: *With Prince Charles at Klosters; although co-operative on this occasion, Diana has been known to become furiously angry with intrusive photographers when she is skiing.*

RIGHT: *The Princess with the Duke and Duchess of York, all well muffled up against the biting cold.*

FAR RIGHT: *Returning exhausted after a long day on the ski slopes, the Princess will be fully recovered in a few hours and ready for some nightlife.*

One holiday taste that the Princess does share with her husband is skiing. Together with a group of friends, they made annual visits to Klosters in the Swiss Alps, until the tragic accident in 1988 when Major Hugh Lindsay, former equerry to the Queen and a good friend of both the Prince and Princess of Wales, was killed by an avalanche. The Princess learned to ski as a teenager and, while not a daredevil skier like her husband or the Duchess of York, enjoys both the sport and the *après-ski* social life that is an integral part of it. Although Prince Charles has been back to Klosters since 1988, the Princess has stayed away. Her most recent skiing holiday, in March 1992 at Lech in Austria, with Charles, and the two boys, was also tragically interrupted by the news of her father's death.

ABOVE, RIGHT AND FAR RIGHT: *Holidays with the Spanish royal family at the Marivent Palace on Majorca have become a regular feature of the summer and are far more to Diana's taste than the hearty outdoor life of Balmoral. Diana and the boys enjoy the beach and pool, while Charles is more inclined to drive up into the hills for some sketching.*

ABOVE: *In carefree mood at Marivent Palace,
though the sunshine seems to be getting to Harry.
Prince Charles and Queen Sofia of Spain are in
the background.*

RIGHT: *Not many women are so trim in a bikini
after two pregnancies.*

OVERLEAF: *In April 1990 Diana and her sons shared
a private beach holiday in the British Virgin
Islands with her mother, Mrs Shand Kydd, and two
sisters, Lady Jane Fellowes and Lady Sarah
McCorquodale, plus assorted nephews and nieces.
Clearly a good time was had by all.*

Necker Isla
PRIVATE
NO ENTRY
for Information
4·2757 - 4·4492
.We Monitor C

CHAPTER 5

CARING PRINCESS: CHARITY AND ARTS WORK

ABOVE: *In her role as patron of the charity Help the Aged, Diana visits Bridges community project in Gwent.*

RIGHT: *The prize-giving and graduation ceremony of the Royal Academy of Music, held at St Marylebone's Church.*

As the attraction of dressing up and simply being admired began to pall, Diana became a career princess, increasingly aware of her high-profile value as a fund-raiser and charity patron. This is not, however, a totally new departure for her; the boarding school she attended in her early teens, West Heath in Kent, encouraged its pupils to become involved in the local community. Diana and a friend regularly visited an old lady in Sevenoaks, doing some housework and shopping for her, and she also worked for the local Voluntary Service Unit, visiting mentally and physically handicapped patients at a local hospital.

Initially Diana's work as patron was mainly in the arts field; she counts RADA (the Royal Academy of Dramatic Arts), the Royal Academy of Music and the English National Ballet among the imposing bodies of which she is President. Rather more surprising is her role as Colonel-in-Chief of a number of regiments. After the assassination of Lord Mountbatten, she was invited to succeed him as Colonel-in-Chief of the Royal Hampshires, the last royal line regiment affiliated to a single county. She is also Colonel-in-Chief of the 13/18th Royal Hussars and the Princess of Wales Own Regiment of Canada, and Honorary Commandant, RAF Wittering, which entails reading massive folders of papers on defence issues.

A more personal sense of involvement is reflected in the work the Princess does for family-related charities. One of her earliest commitments in this field was to Dr

ABOVE: *Even on her first official tour to Wales in 1981, Diana proved that she had a natural way with children. Ten years later the passionate concern is undiminished, as the Princess visits Great Ormond Street Hospital for Children in March 1991.*

RIGHT: *A Barnardo day care centre in Brixton, south London.*

FAR RIGHT: *Young Sara, aged five, presented the Princess with flowers and was lifted on to the royal lap during a visit to a home for abused children in Kingston, Canada, in October 1991.*

Barnardo's children's homes, of which she has been an extremely active President for over seven years. She has the natural gift of accepting people as they are and putting them at their ease. When Barnardo's asked her to sign a 'Children's Charter', she arranged for three mentally handicapped children to join the ceremony in the Waleses' Kensington Palace apartment, and responded cheerfully to an off-the-cuff request for a guided tour. While her role as president may give a wonderful boost to fund-raising, it is individual visits that give most pleasure, and the Princess is as generous with her time as with her purse.

She makes a point of keeping abreast of family-related issues that hit the headlines. One such issue was that of child abuse, sparked by the controversial diagnosis of multiple abuse in a large number of families in Cleveland, northern England. As a result Diana became involved with Childline, a charity established by television personality Esther Rantzen to offer abused children a confidential telephone help and advice service. On a number of visits the Princess has sat and listened as volunteers man the phones and has heard some horrifying tales. As well as making substantial donations herself, her involvement and interest has helped to raise the charity's profile and increase the flow of funds.

By far her most significant role, however, has been the support she has given to less obviously popular and high-profile charities. When she visited a purpose-built ward for Aids sufferers in April 1987, at a time when there was a considerable public hysteria about the disease, her gesture achieved more than any government education programme. She met nine terminally ill men, shook their hands, sat on their beds and talked to them about their condition in a way that medical staff, not normally noted for their susceptibility, found 'very moving'.

Diana's close involvement in Aids fund-raising and counselling has required considerable personal bravery in facing the social taboos surrounding a disease with no cure. The death in 1991 from Aids of a close friend, Adrian Ward-Jackson, well known for his work in the arts world, has reinforced this commitment. She has now taken on the role of patron to the National Aids Trust, making her first appearance in that capacity in April 1991 with a speech she wrote herself: 'HIV does not make people dangerous to know, so you can shake hands and give them a hug – heaven knows they need it.' Some months earlier she had flown to Washington DC on a one-day fund-raising trip and made a point of visiting a home for children with Aids, an experience that left more than one of her staff close to tears.

The Princess's growing interest in and commitment to the charities with which she works has extended into the wider implications of the social issues that they raise. She has tried to focus on this in speeches on family life, drug

and alcohol abuse and the problems of old age, but is still a nervous and hesitant speechmaker. Film director Sir Richard Attenborough has been an encouraging coach, teaching her to take a slow breath at the end of each sentence so that she does not speak too fast, and telling her when to smile or raise her head, so that the speech flows in a natural rhythm.

Another cause that is close to her heart is drug abuse, and she has hosted a reception at Kensington Palace for Turning Point, a charity which concerns itself with both drug and alcohol abuse. Interestingly, she was more hesitant about becoming involved with the marriage guidance counselling service Relate, turning down the first approach to become its patron. Since becoming Princess of Wales she has been approached for support by well over two hundred organizations and takes care to be selective. The negative response to Relate was accompanied by an offer to visit their headquarters in Rugby to learn more about their operation. She was sufficiently impressed to become actively involved in counselling sessions. When Relate approached her again she was happy to agree, and has since attended private role-play sessions for trainee counsellors, where her sympathetic interaction prompted Relate's director to describe her as 'perceptive and intuitive . . . she would make a very good addition to our team because she is such a natural communicator.'

The image of the do-gooding aristocrat is both an attractive and a contentious one, and swiftly becomes as clichéd as the phrase 'Caring Princess.' When the magazine *Vanity Fair* described her as a saint, other journalists sharpened their axes, and the Princess herself was mortally embarrassed; being put on a pedestal or hailed as an angel of mercy on the basis of short visits and natural charm in her view devalues the work of those many committed workers who can and do devote themselves full-time to the causes which she supports. But she also knows, as one Aids patient told her, that 'One handshake from you is worth more than a million words from us.'

ABOVE: *At an earlier visit to Great Ormond Street Hospital for Children, Diana still sports the longer hairstyle she wore for her wedding.*

RIGHT: *Undaunted by the weather on a visit to a project being carried out by Oldham and Rochdale groundwork trust at Princess Park, Oldham.*

RIGHT: *The Princess gets closely involved at the International Deaf Youth Rally in South Glamorgan. When asked to address an international convention for the deaf, she delighted her audience by 'signing' her speech.*

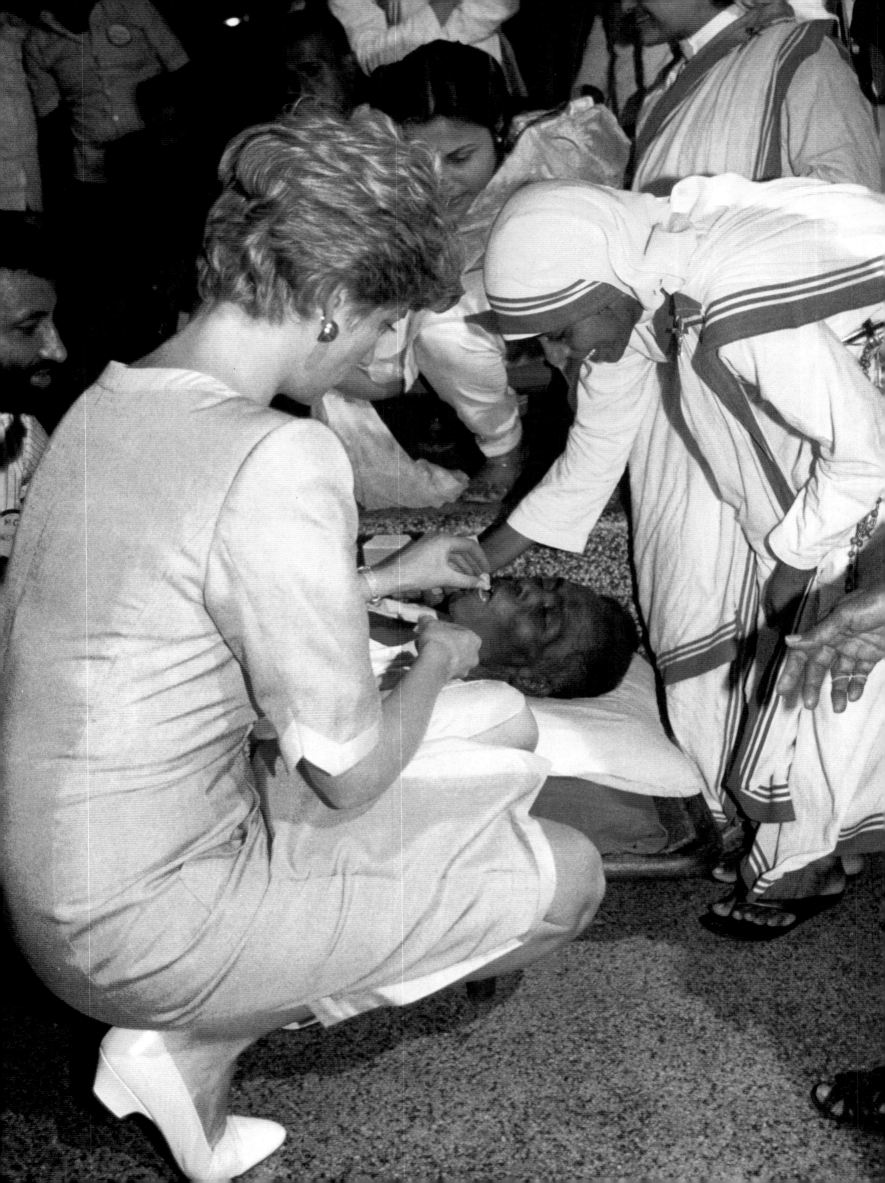

LEFT: *The twentieth-century equivalent of the medieval belief that a king's touch could cure? Princess Diana feeds a dying man during a visit to Mother Theresa's Hospice for the Dying, Calcutta, in February 1992.*

RIGHT: *Some of Diana's most important charity work has concerned AIDS. Here she opens an AIDS ward at Middlesex Hospital.*

BELOW: *When the Waleses went on a five-day official tour of Brazil in April 1991, Diana insisted on including a visit to AIDS patients at the university hospital, Rio de Janeiro.*

LEFT: *Charity galas are an essential and pleasurable feature of the Princess's fund-raising work; here (pregnant with William) she meets screen goddess Elizabeth Taylor after the gala premiere of* Little Foxes *in which Taylor starred.*

RIGHT: *Diana at her most sylphlike is photographed with New Zealand soprano Dame Kiri te Kanawa at a concert in aid of Westminster Children's Hospital.*

BELOW: *Meeting* Dynasty *star Joan Collins and fashion designer Bruce Oldfield at a charity dinner in aid of Dr Barnardo's Children's Homes; the eye-catching gold dress is an Oldfield design.*

PREVIOUS PAGES: *Surrounded by New York's Finest, Diana meets an enthusiastic crowd outside Harlem Hospital, where she visited the paediatric AIDS clinic.*

ABOVE: *During her flying visit to Washington DC, the Princess receives a T-shirt and hat that read 'Spread the word not the virus' as she leaves Grandpa's House, a centre for abandoned and abused children.*

RIGHT: *Diana shakes hands with a leper child at Sitanala leprosy hospital during a four-day visit to Indonesia with Prince Charles. The gesture was a significant one in helping to dispel the continuing folk myths about the disease.*

FAR RIGHT: *Receiving a bouquet of flowers at a HelpAge home in Brussels during a visit to open the new Brussels office of Help the Aged International.*

TOP: *At the Peto Institute, Budapest, Diana chats with Dawn Rogers, who has learned to walk as a result of specialist care.*

ABOVE: *Playing the piano for Czechoslovak orphans at Prague Castle during an official tour.*

RIGHT: *At ease with a five-year-old leukaemia patient at the Ontario Regional Cancer Centre in October 1991.*

CHAPTER 6

A WORKING PRINCESS: STATE AND FORMAL OCCASIONS

RIGHT: *For her first State Opening of Parliament on 4th November 1981, the Princess was the focus of all eyes in her white chiffon dress, tiara and four-strand pearl choker on loan from the Queen. 'She absolutely lit up the old place', said one appreciative MP, but perhaps her husband was less impressed with this subconscious scene-stealing.*

RIGHT: *Photographed with a Gurkha regiment in the Khyber Pass during her first major solo trip to Pakistan, in 1991. This has since proved a significant turning point in Diana's evolution into an independent princess.*

The royal family work to a rigid timetable, planned out in meticulous detail months in advance, and the Princess of Wales is no exception to this rule. When she is in residence in the apartments she still maintains at Kensington Palace, she drives herself to work each morning. The original plan was for Kensington Palace to house the Prince and Princess's office suites as well as their private rooms, and it was Diana who put her foot down at the idea of 'living over the shop.' So she drives herself to work in St James's Palace, pleasantly situated in the heart of London's West End between Green Park and St James's Park, a stone's throw from Buckingham Palace.

Many of Diana's staff are naval officers, who may be commanding frigates one moment and drafting royal speeches the next; they return to sea after a two-year secondment. One royal observer has described them tellingly as 'noted for their short haircuts, gleaming shoes, and the healthy pinkness of people who have had early morning showers. All-Bran, and a run in the park before reaching their desks each morning eager and freshly bright.' The seven ladies-in-waiting form the backbone of the operation, with two or more always in attendance at engagements.

The pace has hotted up in the Princess's offices in the last five or six years, since she began to surround herself with a younger and more dynamic team than the

standard middle-aged royal courtiers. She is now one of the more hard-working of the royals in her own right; the Prince of Wales seems deliberately to have left 'meet the people' engagements to his wife while he concentrates on discussions and working lunches with teams of experts.

The programme is planned at six-monthly intervals in June and December, with equerries, private secretaries, ladies-in-waiting and detectives all involved. Before an engagement is accepted a draft itinerary must be provided; if approved, a detective and an equerry go on a preliminary visit; and the final programme is sent to every department in St James's Palace.

Security is one of the most irksome aspects of royal life. Diana and her staff can never forget that in every crowd may lurk a potential assassin. The constant presence at her side of a bodyguard is an unwelcome reminder of the constraints of her position; even a casual lunch with a friend in a Knightsbridge restaurant is shadowed by a discreet form at a nearby table. An ambulance and a fire engine are on permanent standby.

The Princess's reaction to this ever-present threat has been a characteristically practical one. At the SAS (Special Air Services) headquarters in Hereford she was put through a rigorous anti-terrorist driving course which included avoiding thunderflashes and smoke bombs. She is now an extremely fast and competent driver, being

flagged down more than once by speed police on her journeys between Highgrove and London. She has also attended the Metropolitan Police weapons' training centre, where she was taught to use a .38 caliber Smith and Wesson revolver and machine pistol.

There are some obligatory fixed points in the royal calendar, known to insiders as 'MOBG' – morally obliged to go. These include the Trooping of the Colour, the Queen's official birthday parade on the second Saturday in June. This, a major review of the Queen's ceremonial troops on Horse Guards Parade in central London, is one of the most spectacular displays of pageantry in the world. The Braemar Highland Games at the beginning of September is one of the few public occasions for which the Queen breaks her Balmoral summer holiday, and her guests are also expected to attend. November brings both the State Opening of Parliament, where monarchy meets democracy in another elegant and colourful ceremony, and the more sombre Remembrance Day parade.

It is the royal tours, however, which both attract the most media attention and require the most detailed and arduous planning. The first major tour for the fledgling Princess was Australia in 1982, shortly after the birth of Prince William. It was staggeringly successful, but its very success made it a punishing endurance test. Out of a population of 17 million, around one million of those turned out to see the royal couple, and at times the welcome bordered on hysteria. No one in the royal party, let alone the inexperienced Diana, had met this kind of reception before, and it was Diana the crowds wanted; when they got Prince Charles on their side of the streets

during the numerous royal walkabouts, they complained bitterly. This was the first manifestation of the now familiar phenomenon of Princess as Megastar; if seasoned courtiers were taken aback, the unfortunate Diana was devastated, and would weep with nervous exhaustion at the end of yet another long, exposed day.

Since those early days she has adapted with charm and efficiency to the peculiar rhythm of royal tours, described by one royal newshound as 'a combination of stultifying boredom, sublime settings, and ridiculous red tape.' A sense of humour certainly helps to cope with the elaborate absurdities laid on by over-enthusiastic locals – like the bare earth painted green in Halifax, Nova Scotia, to match the specially laid turf. Sumptuousness reached its peak in the Gulf in 1986, where the Princess was given several gorgeous suites of jewellery, including a diamond choker nearly two inches wide from the Emir of Kuwait. In Saudi Arabia their hosts transferred the entire contents of a palace into the desert, Persian carpets and all, so that the royal couple could enjoy a typically Arab desert banquet. Amid all the glamour, however, the Princess never forgets that each visit has a purpose: the Gulf tour was to encourage investment in British expertise.

Other major royal tours have included Washington in 1985; Canada in 1986 to open Expo 86 in Vancouver; West Germany in 1987; Paris and the Far East in 1988; Nigeria, Italy and Japan in 1990; and India and the ill-fated Korean tour in 1992. 1991 saw a new departure, with the Princess going on her first major solo trip, to Pakistan, and in March 1992 she instituted another innovation, taking her sister Sarah to Budapest in the role of lady-in-waiting.

LEFT: *Dressed for the heat in Luxor, Egypt, spring 1992.*

ABOVE: *Dressed for the cold with President Vaclav Havel of Czechoslovakia at a war cemetery in Prague, spring 1991.*

ABOVE AND ABOVE RIGHT: *Two very different forms of entertainment on the Gulf tour: a desert banquet and a formal feast.*

RIGHT: *Rubbing noses is a traditional Maori greeting: New Zealand.*

FAR RIGHT: *A typically romantic Spanish gesture welcomes the Princess on a formal visit to Madrid.*

ABOVE: *The visit that the Prince and Princess of Wales made to Italy in 1985 caused controversy at home. Prince Charles had been in correspondence with Pope John Paul and had arranged for them to attend privately a personal Mass in the Vatican. The idea of the heir to the English throne, the future Head of the Church of England, attending a Catholic service was too much for the forces of conservatism and the couple had to cancel, but still enjoyed a private audience with the Pontiff.*

RIGHT: *The royal couple pay their respects during Commonwealth Remembrance Day ceremonies in Yokohama. They visited Japan for the coronation of Emperor Akihito.*

ABOVE: *The Venetian gondolas take particular pride in ferrying their royal cargo.*

FAR LEFT: *During her visit to Japan for the imperial coronation, Diana was photographed trying on a kimono.*

LEFT: *The Prince and Princess of Wales looking happy and relaxed in Germany in 1989, at the height of media speculation about the state of their marriage.*

FAR LEFT: *Diana's visit to the ancient and landlocked kingdom of Nepal, high in the Himalayas, followed soon after the announcement of her separation from Prince Charles.*

LEFT AND BELOW: *At this meet-the-people function organized by the Nepalese Red Cross, Diana combines two of her best-loved roles, as career princess and as warm-hearted charity patron.*

ABOVE: *On her solo trip to Paris in spring 1993, Diana met Paul and Linda McCartney, lunched with film star Gerard Dépardieu, and totally captivated the susceptible French.*

LEFT: *Meeting the corps de ballet at the Paris Opéra.*

LEFT: *Every inch the modern princess. After more press comment and publicity, both critical and favourable, than any one person should be expected to bear, Diana seems to have found a resilience and an equilibrium that should carry her gracefully through whatever stresses and surprises the years may bring.*

Index

Figures in *italics* refer to
illustrations and diagrams.

Acknowledgments

The publisher would like to thank Mike Rose of Casebourne Rose for
designing this book and Helen Dawson for indexing it. We would also like
to thank the following individuals, institutions and agencies for supplying
illustrative material.

Bettmann Archive: pages 11 (below right), 12 (right), 14, 16 (above), 19
  (above), 41, 43 (below), 59
Bettmann/Hulton Collection: page 11 (left)
Hulton Deutsch Collection: pages 6, 8 (right), 9 (both), 10, 62, 63, 64
  (bottom), 70 (both), 71
Anwar Hussein: pages 1, 2, 4, 7, 8 (left), 11 (top right), 12 (left), 13, 15
  (both), 16 (below), 17, 18 (both), 19 (below), 20, 21, 22, 23 (both), 24,
  25, 26, 27 (both), 28, 29, 30 (all three), 31, 32, 33 (all three), 34 (all
  three), 35, 36, 37, 38, 39, 40, 42, 43 (above), 45, 46 (bottom), 48, 49, 50,
  51, 52 (both), 53, 54 (both), 55, 56 (all three), 57, 58, 64 (top), 69 (top),
  78, 79, 80, 81 (all three), 82/3, 84, 85, 86 (both), 87 (both), 88, 90, 91
  (both), 92, 93 (both), 94, 95 (both)
Reuters/Bettmann Newsphotos: pages 44, 45 (top), 47, 60, 61, 65, 68, 69
  (bottom), 72/3, 74 (both), 75, 76 (both), 77, 89